Dealing With Giants

Taking on the Problem of Internet Pornography

TONY HOFFMAN

Copyright © 2010 Tony Hoffman

All rights reserved.

ISBN: 1456559877
ISBN-13: 978-1456559878

DEDICATION

Teresa—I love you and thank God for you each day.

CONTENTS

1	Dealing With Giants	1
2	A Brief History of Pornography in America	13
3	The Next Sexual Revolution	23
4	The Problem of Internet Pornography	31
5	Internet Pornography and Women	53
6	Internet Pornography and the Church	61
7	Godly Leadership	75
8	Take Action	81
	Appendix 1: "S"	89
	Appendix 2: SOAP Bible Study Method	93
	Notes	111

CHAPTER 1
DEALING WITH GIANTS

I have always liked the Biblical account of Caleb. Moses sent Caleb and Joshua along with ten other men to explore Canaan in preparation for their journey into the land. The explorers were to go up into the hill country to see what the land was like. Were the people there strong or weak, few or many? Were the cities unwalled or fortified? How is the soil? Is it fertile or poor? How good is the fruit of the land?

The explorers journeyed into the land until they came to the region of Hebron. There they found fertile land and good fruit, but they also found the descendants of Anak—giant fierce warriors who made them tremble with fear. The explorers returned to Moses where only Joshua and Caleb suggested they should attempt to take the land. The other ten explorers believed the dangers of the land too powerful to overcome. These ten men convinced the Israelites to turn back in fear and they refused to enter the Promised Land. As a result, the Israelites spent forty years wandering in the desert.

When Joshua finally led them into Canaan, the Israelites began occupying the land, but no one, it seemed, was willing to take on the challenge of the hill country where the giant descendants of Anak lived. Was there anyone among the people of God willing to face the giants? Faithful Caleb was willing, and he stepped up to Joshua and said,

> *I was forty years old when Moses the servant of the LORD sent me from Kadesh Barnea to explore the land. And I brought him back a report according to my convictions, but my brothers who went up with me made the hearts of the people melt with fear. I, however, followed the LORD my God wholeheartedly. So on that day Moses swore to me, 'The land on which your feet have walked will be your inheritance and that of your children*

> *forever, because you have followed the LORD my God wholeheartedly.'*
>
> *"Now then, just as the LORD promised, he has kept me alive for forty-five years since the time he said this to Moses, while Israel moved about in the desert. So here I am today, eighty-five years old! I am still as strong today as the day Moses sent me out; I'm just as vigorous to go out to battle now as I was then. Now give me this hill country that the LORD promised me that day. You yourself heard then that the Anakites were there and their cities were large and fortified, but, the LORD helping me, I will drive them out just as he said."*
>
> Joshua 14:6-15 (NIV)

There was a job to do. Giants were still in the land and someone needed to deal with them. Caleb believed that he was called by God to take on those giants, and with God's help he drove them from the land and the people had peace.

Once again, there is a job to do. Internet pornography threatens our society and our families. It is a multi-billion dollar industry with powerful allies in government and business, and its secret and efficient distribution system can reach instantly into any home with a computer. Internet pornography is a giant that few seem willing to deal with.

Internet Pornography

In recent years, the Internet has significantly impacted life in America. Seventy-seven percent of people living in the United States are Internet users.[1] The Internet has affected the way Americans work, learn, shop, communicate, entertain, and relate to one another. One of the most significant and pervasive influences of the Internet, however, is in the way it has transformed how Americans think about and participate in sexuality.

The Internet, while originally developed by the military as a communication tool in the event of a nuclear disaster, quickly expanded into academic, business, and private arenas.[2] In the early 1980s when the World Wide Web was established, pornography producers, who historically have been quick to embrace new technologies as potential outlets for distribution, invested heavily in developing an online presence. The growth of online pornography has been truly staggering. Al Cooper, the late researcher with the San Jose Marital and Sexuality Center, estimated that 70% of all money spent for online content is used for sexually explicit materials. In addition, Cooper found that nearly 18 million people in the United States accessed pornography online in 2000 and that approximately 20% of Internet users were involved in online sexual behavior.[3] In December 2005, only 5 years after Al Cooper's findings, the number of Internet users accessing pornography online more than tripled to over 60 million.[4]

The prevalence of Internet pornography has raised concerns among both government officials and mental health professionals. In addition, church leaders are beginning to recognize the dangers of sexually explicit materials on the Internet. While it might be expected that participation in Christian life and faith, would render a person less susceptible to the lure of Internet pornography, studies have shown that this is not necessarily the case. A Christianity Today survey revealed that approximately one-third of Christian laity and clergy have visited sexually explicit Internet sites, with 18% of clergy visiting them on repeated occasions.[5] In addition, a recent study published in the Journal of Psychology and Theology found that Internet pornography showed a statistically significant positive correlation with religiosity scores in a sample of undergraduate male college students. This was a surprising discovery considering that religiosity has been demonstrated to be associated with lower rates of other problematic behaviors such as alcohol, gambling, and drug use.[6]

The relatively high rate of Internet pornography use among religious people, especially those within the Christian church in America, raises a number of issues that need addressing. Al Cooper, who was one of the first researchers to study Internet pornography, suggests that Internet pornography may be fueled by a Triple-A-Engine of **Accessibility**—can be accessed anytime and almost anywhere, **Affordability**—very inexpensive or even free, and **Anonymity**—perception that no one else knows what one is doing.[7] This Triple-A-Engine bypasses the typical social boundaries normally associated with pornography: shopping at an adult book or video store, ordering explicit material through the mail, or going to an adult theater.

With the aid of the Internet, anyone by simply clicking a computer mouse, can obtain the most sexually explicit material in the privacy of his own home or office. These factors seem to contribute to the lure of online pornography and have resulted in Internet pornography's rapid intrusion into the American culture and the American church.

A Battle for the Church

Historically, churches in the United States have been unwilling to simply accept the production and distribution of pornography, and their fight against this social ill has been a truly ecumenical endeavor. When the Catholic Church in the United States established the Legion of Decency in 1934 to review motion pictures and to pressure Hollywood to remove objectionable content, it found ready allies among American Protestants.[8] In more recent times, churches have banned together to help establish the current motion picture rating system, protest adult bookstores and theaters, and fight the distribution of pornography, especially child pornography.

Many denominations have also gone on record to condemn the use of pornography and to call for social action against it. The following churches are among those issuing official statements condemning pornography in America: Roman Catholic, American Baptist, Baptist General Conference, Christian Church, Christian Reformed, Church of God in Christ, Church of the Brethren, Church of the Nazarene, Episcopal, Evangelical Congregational, Evangelical Free Church of America, Evangelical Lutheran Church of America, Free Methodist,

Greek Orthodox, Independent Fundamental Churches of America, Lutheran Church-Missouri Synod, National Association of Free Will Baptists, Churches of Christ, Presbyterian Church U.S.A., Reformed Church in America, Salvation Army, Seventh-day Adventist, Southern Baptist Convention, United Church of Christ, United Methodist, and Wesleyan.[9]

Surprisingly, however, the American Church's fight against pornography has largely been outwardly focused, consisting of legislative and social action aimed at stopping the production and distribution of pornography. While these efforts have undoubtedly resulted in some local and temporary victories, the current prevalence of pornography indicates that the outwardly focused fight has been largely ineffective. If the church is going to engage effectively in the fight against pornography, then it must focus primarily, not on outward legislative and social action, but on the inward spiritual battle, where pornography assaults the mind and spirit.

Not a Legislative or Social Battle

The problem of Internet pornography will not be solved by legislation or social action. In 1998, Congress passed the Child Online Protection Act, or COPA, in an attempt to protect children from the harmful effects of Internet pornography. The law, however, was immediately challenged in the courts by pornography and freedom of speech advocates and was never enacted. The Supreme Court on January 21, 2009, refused to hear appeals from the lower courts, and effectively killed the bill. The courts chose to embrace pornography as a freedom of speech issue instead of protecting America's youth. The failure to pass COPA demonstrates the need to engage the battle against Internet pornography on a front other than legislation.

In addition, the problem of Internet Pornography will not be effectively addressed with social action. In the past, citizens concerned with the growing presence of adult bookstores or erotic entertainment venues in their neighborhoods put pressure on these businesses through protests, petitions, and other direct social action. Internet pornography, however, is distributed anonymously online directly into homes and offices making it a very difficult target for social action.

With the legislative fight wavering, and the social action fight robbed of its most effective weaponry, another front must be established in the battle against Internet pornography. Fortunately, the spiritual arena offers an effective strategy and a powerful arsenal to help stem the tide of Internet pornography's progress.

A Spiritual Battle

The spiritual arena may be the most effective arena for the church to engage the fight against Internet pornography. Because of the effective and immediate distribution system provided by the Internet, pornography has very few barriers it must overcome to enter hearts and minds. There are no outer social barriers of visiting an adult book or video store, and few if any financial barriers to deter Internet pornography use. The only real barriers left for halting the advance of Internet pornography are inner personal and spiritual barriers.

The best chance to win the fight against Internet pornography is to develop a process that helps individuals build inner barriers in their lives that provide a formidable defense against the temptation to consume Internet pornography. Thankfully, the church has powerful weapons at its disposal that can effectively defend against Internet pornography.

DEALING WITH GIANTS

For though we live in the world, we do not wage war as the world does. The weapons we fight with are not the weapons of the world. On the contrary, they have divine power to demolish strongholds.

2 Corinthians 10:3-4 (NIV)

We need divine power to demolish the stronghold of Internet pornography. For too long, the church relied on worldly weapons to deal with the problem of Internet Pornography. It is now time to bring out the big guns. It is time to rely on God's power. In a later chapter we will discuss how to engage in this battle with spiritual weapons.

CHAPTER 2
A BRIEF HISTORY OF PORNOGRAPHY IN AMERICA

Internet pornography did not merely appear without warning on the American scene, but was the result of a progression of historical events that built one upon another over a period spanning nearly two centuries. To gain a better understanding of Internet pornography in the American cultural context, it may be helpful to explore the introduction and development of pornography in America.

Pornography, at least in the beginning, was mostly imported by European immigrants.[1] The earliest pornographic expressions during the colonial period consisted of pornographic playing cards, carved objects, music boxes, prints, and books. As the trade in pornography grew, some states began passing legislation to prohibit the dissemination of such materials. In 1711, Massachusetts passed such legislation aimed primarily at material deemed antireligious or blasphemous.[2] Eventually, other states also began passing similar legislation.

The first actual trial for obscenity in the United States was in 1815 in Pennsylvania.[3] Apparently, several men had solicited payment in exchange for viewing a sexually explicit painting. As a whole, there were relatively few official prosecutions for pornography before the middle of the nineteenth century.[4] The first federal legislation against pornography was enacted in 1842 when congress passed a tariff to curtail the importation of nude postcards and obscene books primarily from France and other European countries. "The Tariff Act of 1842, in effect, made the Customs Bureau the nation's chief censor, with wide powers. The bureau could interdict or destroy imported materials without first seeking a judicial determination of obscenity".[5]

The Domestic Pornography Industry

While the Tariff Act was intended to reduce the distribution of obscene and pornographic material, its primary impact was to cause an increase in domestic pornography production. In effect, the Tariff Act functioned to protect the fledgling American pornography market from foreign competitors. Most of the domestic pornography during the mid-nineteenth century consisted of salacious novels such as those written by George Lippard, who sold more than 300,000 copies between 1844 and 1854. The large profits witnessed by these first American pornographers spurred the development of a national pornography trade with publishing houses springing up in Philadelphia, Boston, New Orleans, and other population centers.[6]

The mid-nineteenth century also witnessed the establishment of another type of pornography in the form of live erotic shows. Traveling fairs and carnivals of the period introduced "strip shows" and other types of erotic performance.[7] The financial success of these traveling shows led to the eventual establishment of permanent locations that featured live erotic shows.

The invention of photography, however, was undoubtedly most instrumental in establishing pornography in America. In 1839, Louis Daguerre introduced his daguerreotype, and only a few years later pornographic daguerreotype plates began appearing. This demonstrates a phenomenon called Slade's Law which states that whenever a new communication technology appears, someone will invent a sexual use for it.[8] Slade's Law has been demonstrated time and again with the development of new technologies: printing, photography, film, VCR and DVD recordings, computers, the Internet, and smart phones.

The new boost in the pornography market in the latter half of the nineteenth century brought about through the invention of photography, was accompanied by a renewed emphasis in the fight against such material. Anthony Comstock was perhaps the most influential leader in the fight against public obscenity. The Comstock Act of 1873 prohibited sending pornographic and obscene materials through the mail and was later amended to prohibit indecent radio communication.[9] The following discussion will explore how the changing legal and political climate in America created a ready environment for the emergence of a lucrative and powerful pornography industry in America.

Pornography in a Changing Legal Climate

Much of the legal climate in the late nineteenth and early twentieth centuries in America concerning pornographic material was based on an English legal precedent established in Regina v. Hicklin in 1868. "In this case, an English court ruled that a work was obscene if it tended to corrupt and deprave minds that were open to such immoral influence and into whose hands the material might fall".[10] The Hicklin ruling greatly influenced American law and, for the most part, rendered obscenity and pornography illegal until 1957 when it was challenged and the precedent overturned in Roth v. United States. This ruling took an absolutist view of the First Amendment stating the government should not prohibit speech or publication even if such speech or publication might have an undesirable impact. Roth v. United States in effect opened the doors for the legal commercialization of pornography in every conceivable medium and with almost any conceivable content, and has been upheld against challenges in 1973, 1976, 1986 and 1987.[11]

Following the historic ruling in Roth v. United States there was a period that has been called the Sexual Revolution which spanned the late 1950s and 1960s.[12] During this period, the production of pornography greatly increased, and modern popular artists began filling galleries with sexually explicit, obscene, and bizarre photographs, sculptures, and paintings. The sexual candor instigated by the Sexual Revolution had a limited public backlash and resulted in some tightening of obscenity regulations. In 1969, the New York Times published an editorial called "Beyond the Garbage Pale," in which the editors expressed concern over the increasingly obscene nature of pornography and live sex shows in New York.[13]

Even with the backlash, however, public sexual expression and the distribution of pornography continued to increase with greater explicitness in what was portrayed.[14] In addition, the courts continued to take an increasingly libertarian position when dealing with obscenity and pornography.

President's Commission on Obscenity and Pornography

In 1967, President Johnson established the first President's Commission on Obscenity and Pornography to explore the issues surrounding the so called Sexual Revolution and the increased production and distribution of pornographic materials. "The commission gathered the largest corpus of research ever assembled on pornography in nine volumes of technical reports, but its real function was to dramatize the Sexual Revolution that had swept across the United States".[15]

In 1970, the commission issued its final report recommending that federal, state, and local legislation prohibiting the sale, exhibition, or distribution of sexual materials to consenting adults should be repealed. The commission report was based on research claiming that there was no evidence that sexually explicit materials caused any significant harm to individuals or society.[16] The United States Senate eventually rejected the commission's report by a sixty to five vote, and President Nixon denounced its conclusions, calling them morally bankrupt.[17] Despite being rejected by both the president and the senate, the commission's report combined with an increasingly libertarian position of the courts helped to further deteriorate both legal and cultural resistance to pornography. This progressive deterioration of resistance to pornography established a cultural climate favorable to the introduction of Internet pornography. When Internet pornography was finally introduced, it found a broad audience primed and ready to embrace it.

The Attorney General's Commission on Pornography

There were some indications, however, that a segment of American society was not willing to readily accept pornography in any form. In 1985, President Reagan, under pressure to address the problem of pornography, convened the Attorney General's Commission on Pornography which was also called the Meese Commission. This commission released its final report in 1986 and was widely regarded as an attempted counter to the liberal findings of the Johnson Commission. The Meese Commission concluded that violent forms of pornography had the potential to cause harmful effects and were becoming more prevalent. As a result of these conclusions, the commission called for the expansion of existing obscenity statutes. While the Meese Commission report supported tightening regulations against obscenity and pornography, the courts repeatedly overturned attempts to enact such legal changes.[18] As a whole, because of the intervention of the courts, the Meese Commission did little to stem the tide of obscene and pornographic material that was increasingly saturating American society. This intervention of the courts protected pornography in America and established the view that pornography was primarily about freedom of speech. This view trumped all other views concerning pornography, including, protection of American youth, morality, and community problems associated with the production and distribution of obscene media, and set the stage for rapid expansion of the pornography industry.

3 THE NEXT SEXUAL REVOLUTION

The Internet has been referred to as the next Sexual Revolution, as the astonishing growth of computers and technology and the rapid expansion of technology have provided an unrivaled medium for sexual expression and communication, and distribution of sexual information of every sort.[1] From its beginning, the Internet seemed to be uniquely suited for the propagation of sexually explicit material. In 1983 the World Wide Web was established, and only two years later commentaries and warnings began appearing concerning pornography's presence online.[2] By the early 1990s, the growing problem of online pornography instigated a debate concerning whether the Internet was a valuable asset or a societal problem.

Internet Pornography

The Internet has helped change the way Americans think about and access pornography. Pornography was once limited in its reach by the printing or production process, delivery of the produced medium, and physical distribution through stores or other outlets. The Internet effectively removes these barriers, enabling pornographers to produce and distribute pornographic material instantly as demand dictates.

The Internet possesses unique characteristics that make it appealing for both pornography producers and consumers. Al Cooper, was the first to identify these unique characteristics, which he called the Internet's Triple-A-Engine of **Accessibility**—can be accessed anytime and almost anywhere, **Affordability**—very inexpensive or even free, and **Anonymity**—perception that no one else knows what one is doing.[3] These three characteristics combine to make the Internet a particularly effective medium for producing and using pornography.

Accessibility

The first key characteristic of Internet pornography is accessibility. Accessibility refers to the ease at which virtually anyone can access pornography online. Nearly 80% of Americans use the Internet and almost half of them do so through broadband connections.[4] The increase in Internet usage, connection speed, and media quality is providing unprecedented opportunities to access pornography online.

Along with the growth of the Internet itself, the presence of online pornography has also experienced a dramatic increase. In 2006, Philip Stark, a professor of Statistics at the University of California, Berkeley, submitted an analysis of Internet content filtering in court, on behalf of the federal government's effort to sustain the Child Online Protection Act (COPA). Stark found an estimated 264 million sexually explicit web documents indexed on the World Wide Web with approximately half of these originating from within the United States.[5] In addition, a recent study by the Kaiser Family Foundation found that 70% of fifteen to seventeen year old youth admitted to inadvertently stumbling upon pornography online, and 23% say this happens "somewhat" or "very" regularly.[6]

A primary reason for inadvertent exposure to online pornography stems from the nature of the pornographic website industry. Many pornographic websites are free and serve as bait to lure people into the commercial websites. In addition, online pornographers use tactics to lure Internet users to their sites such as pop up ads, e-mail spam, and domain names that are similar to those of frequently used non-pornographic websites. Explicit content on the Internet is not segregated into a backroom like in some video stores or labeled like in a bookstore, and it can be difficult to avoid. Sexually explicit imagery is easy to stumble upon online, and a person does not have to be all that active in exploring the Internet to accidently run across sexual material. For those who desire intentionally to seek out pornography, the Internet provides instant access to a virtually unlimited amount and variety of sexually explicit material, twenty four hours a day, seven days a week.

Affordability

With computers and Internet access becoming increasingly more affordable, virtually everyone who desires to do so can gain access to the World Wide Web. Once on the web, a nearly inexhaustible supply of free pornography is available. Even the pay pornographic sites, which charge membership fees to access, are less expensive than traditional forms of print or video media.

Anonymity

The perception of being anonymous while online may encourage some Internet users who would otherwise not view pornography to seek it out on the web. Patrick Carnes, Clinical Director of Sexual Disorders Services at the Meadows in Wickenburg, Arizona, believes anonymity to be a huge factor in online sexual behavior. According to Carnes, people can be anyone they want on the Internet. They don't risk being seen going to an adult video or book store, since they can get all of the pornography they can handle in the privacy of their own homes. The risk of being discovered is low.[7] Compared with offline pornography use, the Internet provides a level of anonymity and secrecy that may actually encourage Internet users to seek out and consume pornography.

The Power of the Internet

The Internet opened up America to pornography in a way no other medium has been able to. The Triple-A-Engine of accessibility, affordability, and anonymity has not only fueled production of pornography, but has also been a primary factor in increasing demand for it.

In a study reported in 2008, 93% of boys and 62% of girls were exposed to Internet pornography before the age of 18.[8] This increased exposure to pornography at an early age is being blamed for much of the increased demand for Internet pornography and the growth of the online pornography industry.

Getting Hooked

In a recent study with male Christian college students who were struggling with Internet pornography addiction, all of the students indicated that the Internet helped them to watch pornography because of its availability and easy access.[9] These students all agreed that the more

Internet pornography they consumed, the more they wanted, and the less they were satisfied.

The Internet takes pornography viewing to a whole new level. The immediate and inexpensive access and the variety of content available on the Internet fuels a desire to consume pornography in increasing doses. A Christian college student explained that because the Internet provided a really private way of viewing pornography it actually encouraged him to seek out and begin to view sexually explicit material.[10] Another student told how he just went online, put in a few search terms, and in his own words, he had his whole world right there. This young man said he was attracted to Internet pornography because it was free, easy, and discreet.[11]

The Internet makes pornography free, easy, and discreet, and provides access to sexually explicit media for a much larger audience than was available with previous distribution methods. This increased access through the Internet, combined with the sexual nature of the content has contributed to increased demand for Internet pornography and the growth and acceptance of the pornography industry.

4 THE PROBLEM OF INTERNET PORNOGRAPHY

Much of the discussion concerning the use of pornography originates from a clinical psychological framework and involves the exploration of psychological causes of pornography use. Because of the nature of the clinical psychological approach, a primary focus in pornography research has been the relationship between individual personality problems, psychological abnormalities, and pornography use.

Pornography use has long been considered deviant and aberrant behavior in the field of Psychology.[1] Pornography on the Internet, however, may be challenging that view. The rapid increase in pornography use due to the Internet is making pornography more mainstream and is transitioning it, at least from the perspective of secular society, out of the realm of deviance. Psychologists who study and counsel pornography users often focus on exploring the psychological factors, such as personality disorders, family history, or biological disorders, that compel individuals to seek out and in some cases become addicted to pornography.[2] These psychological antecedents to pornography use can give insight into the compulsions and addictions related to pornography and help researchers understand the process by which pornography can overcome personal defenses and cause problem behaviors.[3]

Causes of Pornography Use

The search for psychological antecedents to pornography use is valuable if pornography use is an isolated phenomenon. When only a relatively few people in a society use pornography, the question psychologists seek to answer is, "Why do some people use pornography and others do not?" These psychologists then seek to find common factors among the people who use pornography, looking to those factors to explain pornography use.

Since the Internet has helped pornography to become more widely used, even prevalent in some instances, the discussion among psychologists is shifting from what causes the general use of pornography to problematic uses of pornography such as addiction and other specific personal problems.[4] In certain age ranges, it is estimated, that more people use pornography than do not.[5] This extraordinarily high level of Internet pornography use has forced the change in the pornography discussion.

The current discussion coming from the psychological community, concerning pornography, is focused primarily on how to manage problems and consequences of pornography use. There seems to be a growing consensus among psychologists that pornography use is common among the larger population, and that it does not necessarily present a problem unless it turns into addiction, impacts spouses or families, or is accompanied by other problematic behaviors.[6]

Problems and Consequences of Internet Pornography

In 2001, William Fisher and Azy Barak compiled much of the available research concerning factors that affect an individual's choice of sexually explicit material on the Internet.[7] They, suggested that the virtually unlimited range and variety of sexually explicit materials available on the Internet may act to alter the sexual and personal dispositions that incline individuals to seek out Internet sexuality in the first place by reinforcing sexual arousal and stimuli responses associated with online pornography.[8] Fisher and Barak suggest that Internet pornography demonstrates a potential to alter the way a person thinks about sex and responds to sexual stimuli. In addition, because of its wide variety of sexually explicit material—from relatively mundane eroticism to exceptionally bazaar, violent, and antisocial sexual behaviors—Internet pornography can shape an individual's preference concerning the types of sexual stimuli considered desirable. This is especially applicable when that person has little real world sexual experience.

Individual sexual preferences and behavior can be shaped by the Internet when an Internet user is exposed to a sexual stimulus theme that he finds arousing. Over time, the Internet user finds that certain themes in general have become a conditioned erotic stimulus with the capacity to elicit high levels of psychological and physiological sexual arousal and with the ability to motivate sexual behaviors and outcomes.[9] According to these researchers, consistent exposure to Internet pornography possesses the potential to reprogram the human mind with regard to both psychological and physiological responses to sexual stimuli. The Internet then, in some instances, becomes not only an alternative to sexuality and sexual fulfillment, but the only means to achieve sexual fulfillment, especially if a particular learned sexual stimulus is unavailable offline. In these cases, individuals can become dependent on Internet pornography for sexual fulfillment, being unable to experience their preferred sexual stimulus in any other way.

One indicator of this problem might be a sexual disorder called allogynia in men and alloandrism in women, where a person is dependent on sexual fantasy and fantasy partners to stimulate sexual arousal. In these cases the real life sexual partner is insufficient to illicit a sexual response. Researchers and clinicians are finding that some Individuals who experience allogynia or alloandrism may be conditioned to respond to specific sexual stimuli that can only be experienced through the Internet.

Internet Pornography, Brain Science, and Tricks of the Trade

Pornography producers understand how the human brain responds to Internet pornography and they use this knowledge to their advantage. Recent research into how brain chemistry is affected by using Internet pornography can shed light on this problem and may offer some insight into developing effective ways to combat it.

Researchers have discovered that novelty causes certain brain systems, especially the dopamine system, to become activated. The dopamine system sends the neurotransmitter dopamine throughout the various regions of the brain. Dopamine is integral to the pleasure mechanisms of the brain and functions to motivate and reinforce behavior that causes the brain to produce this powerful neurotransmitter.[10]

One of the features that makes Internet pornography so appealing is that it has been shown to be very effective in stimulating the brain to release dopamine. Imagine a young man surfing the Internet and coming across sexually explicit images. There is a good chance that the imagery will cause his brain to react by releasing dopamine as well as a number of other chemicals that cause a pleasurable and powerful psychological and physiological response. In many cases, this response is so pleasing and powerful that the young man is drawn to the imagery time and again in an effort to get more of the same. This is an example of the reward circuitry of the brain at work, and it is one of the most powerful motivators of human behavior.

American marketers understand the value of researching and exploiting what excites the reward circuitry of the brain. The human brain is designed to ignore the old and focus on the new. Marketers, who understand this, will play a television ad for a few weeks, then modify it slightly. These changes are detected by the brain, and the attention of viewers is drawn to the commercial. Novelty is a primary factor in determining what the brain pays attention to. This is where the unique delivery system of the Internet comes into play.

The Internet allows a person to "click through" a large number of images in rapid succession to find the particular ones that activate the brain's reward circuitry. The viewer can then focus on the images that illicit a response, and ignore the images that don't. With the vast amount of explicit sexual media on the Internet anyone can find the imagery that "is right" for his particular reward circuitry.

Pornographers also use their knowledge of the brain's reward circuitry to design tricks to get people hooked on their products. One of these tricks is called "mouse trapping." Mouse trapping is when a person either intentionally or inadvertently opens a pornographic web page, then discovers that any attempt to "click it off" simply opens another pornographic page. Try as he might, the viewer cannot close out the pornography. His efforts to do so only open more and more pornographic pages. The pornography producers are hoping that if the first page doesn't stimulate the brain's reward circuitry, their "mouse trapping" trick will continue to display more images until the reward circuitry is activated. Once this occurs, the brain is flooded with dopamine and other endorphins and its pleasure centers are activated, causing the viewer to crave more.

The manipulation of the brain's reward circuitry is a powerful and compelling motivator for Internet users to continue to seek out Internet pornography. The problem develops as the individual begins viewing pornography more often. His reward circuitry builds up an immunity to the explicit images. The types of imagery that once initiated a response will no longer do it for the viewer. He is forced to seek out newer and more diverse imagery in order to get the same response.

Pornographers understand this as well, and they are ready with a seemingly endless supply of more diverse and even bizarre images for viewers to try. This is when online pornography becomes profitable. Free online pornography is relatively mundane and limited in its content in comparison to what is for sale. When the free content is no longer able to illicit the desired stimulus response, viewers often move to the next step which requires paying for the imagery they need. This is how the addiction develops.

Internet Pornography as Addiction

In 2001, Mark Griffiths summarized much of the available research on Internet sexual addiction.[11] While recognizing the debate concerning the existence of non-chemical addictions such as gambling, pornography, and shopping, Griffiths suggested that compulsive behavior relating to Internet pornography use could be considered a type of addiction. Addiction occurs when viewing Internet pornography becomes the most important activity in the person's life and dominates thinking, feelings, and behavior.[12]

Griffiths' work was based in part on the research of Kimberly Young who considered Internet sexual addiction a classification of Internet addiction. Young described five specific subtypes of Internet addiction. Internet addiction can be Cybersexual addiction which involves the compulsive use of adult websites for cybersex and cyberporn. Cyber-relationship addiction is another form of Internet addiction that involves the over-involvement in online relationships. Another Internet addiction is Net compulsions which involve obsessive/compulsive activeities such as online gambling, shopping, day-trading, online communities, and so forth. Information overload is a fourth type of addiction involving compulsive web surfing or database searching. Finally, computer addiction, involves obsessive computer game playing.[13]

While each of these classifications of Internet addiction involves pathological behaviors associated with Internet use, there is some question as to the specific nature of the affected individual's addiction. In regard to sexually related Internet behavior, is it the sex or the Internet that is the basis for the addiction? Griffiths argues that Internet sex addicts are actually addicted to sex, and that the Internet is merely the place where they engage in the behavior. He does concede however that the Internet possesses certain characteristics that fuel addictive behaviors.

According to Griffiths, the Internet may offer an alternative reality that allows the user feelings of immersion and anonymity. These feelings in themselves may be highly psychologically and/or physiologically rewarding and have been identified as a consistent factor underlying excessive and compulsive uses of the Internet.[14] It is this combination of explicit sexual imagery and the unique qualities of the Internet that give Internet pornography its unique potency and ability to break through personal barriers that would otherwise be sufficient to enable an individual to resist the temptation to view pornography.

Reprogramming the Mind

Addiction to Internet pornography is experienced when an individual's thinking is dominated by the desire to view pornography online.[15] Internet pornography, in essence holds captive the addicted person's mind, making him unable to focus effectively on anything else. Career, school, family, religious commitment, and almost every other area of life is secondary in the mind of the addict.

When dealing with sexual addiction, one of the biggest obstacles an addict must overcome is the visual imagery stored in the brain and the fantasies that continue to dominate thinking. The mind, according to Mark Laaser—a sexual addictions specialist and founder of Faithful and True Ministries—becomes conditioned to think in inappropriate ways and must be retrained. If the mind can be reprogrammed to stop the fantasies, then the behavior triggered by those fantasies can also be changed. Laaser also recommends counseling and maintaining spiritual disciplines in the process of retraining the mind.[16]

Through his research with Christian college students, Huson concluded that addiction and near addictions to Internet pornography can cause an individual to engage in self-deceptive mind tricks that cloud thinking.[17] Huson interviewed 18 male undergraduate college students who identified themselves as born-again Christians and who admitted to having problems with Internet pornography.

Huson found that all of the students in the study wanted to rid their lives of pornography.[18] For these students however, their struggle continues to be ongoing. One student described his struggle as having images in his head that will never go away and will affect him the rest of his life.[19] Another student in the study described how he found a level of success in his struggle by being around Christian men who held him accountable, and by studying the Bible to help refocus his thinking.[20] Throughout Huson's study, the struggle in the mind against pornography is a reoccurring theme. All of the students had a significant level of difficulty dealing with their thoughts about pornography. One students indicated that frequently viewing pornography created a cycle that made him want to view more pornography and masturbate, which in turn made him want to view more pornography. For this student, the only thing that helped to break this cycle was focused spirituality through Christian fellowship and Bible study.[21]

The Internet Generation

Huson's study illustrates the problems of Internet pornography for the generation of young adults who have learned to respond to online sexual stimuli. Those who are currently in college grew up with the Internet, and are likely to have experienced online sexually explicit material from a relatively young age.[22] For these individuals, the current psychological discussion concerning Internet pornography offers limited hope. Many young men who may not be addicted to pornography in the technical sense, and who are not experiencing problems that warrant the interest of the current psychological community, are beginning to realize that their personal lives and relationships are nevertheless being negatively impacted by Internet pornography.

In recent decades, anti-porn activists have called for a ban against pornography, predicting that increased pornography would lead to objectification of women and ultimately to an increase in rape and other types of sexual crime. While experts currently disagree as to the impact pornography has on crimes against women, many are beginning to admit that the proliferation of sexually explicit media online has radically impacted society for the worst.

One example of the negative impact of Internet pornography is that the saturation of children, teens, and young adults with explicit sexual imagery is profoundly affecting the sexuality of young people and making it very difficult for them to have healthy views of sex. Young men and women alike are coming of age with ideas about sex that are so unrealistic that the real thing will never be able to measure up. Some experts are beginning to admit that this distorted view of sex may have incalculable negative consequences for the future of marriages, families, and society.

In a recent article discussing the relationship between Internet pornography and attitudes toward sex, a college student explained how he always tried to have sex as early as possible in a relationship to get it out of the way, and get rid of the tension. For this young man, sex was a given in a relationship; it was biological and mechanical.[23] This college student and millions like him are finding sex commonplace and routine, and some even consider it boring, preferring the fantasy world of Internet pornography to real life sexual relations.

Internet Pornography and the Family

Another issue that is being instigated by the growing presence of Internet pornography in American society is the problem of infidelity through sexual experiences on the Internet.

"Imagine a husband, who would never walk into an adult bookstore, finding out that he could download online pornography cheaply, quickly, and without detection."[24]

Online sexual infidelity is becoming a problem for many couples who may have never had a problem with any other type of sexual unfaithfulness. The power of Internet pornography is a force that is not only destroying lives of American men. It also is destroying American families.

To understand the increased incidence of sexual infidelity online, the ACE model was introduced.

According to the ACE model—anonymity, convenience, and escape—the Internet creates a "culture and climate of permissiveness that encourages and validates sexually adulterous and promiscuous online behavior."[25]

First, the anonymity of the Internet allows an individual to engage in sexual behavior with little fear of being caught. In addition, the lack of physical contact with an actual person gives a sense that the experience is not really infidelity. Many users of Internet pornography do not consider their behavior as being infidelity, though their spouses often do.[26]

In addition to being anonymous, the Internet also provides a very convenient medium for sexual expression and consumption of sexual content. Online sexual behavior occurs in a familiar and comfortable environment of home or office and can become extremely seductive to the point of compulsivity.[27]

Finally, Internet pornography can provide a seemingly harmless escape that has great potential to evolve into a controlling compulsion. More individuals are beginning to turn to sexual behavior online as a release from the stress and pressures of contemporary life. This release provides a level of reinforcement that can lead to addiction.

The evidence for online addiction and compulsivity is growing among helping professionals. Internet pornography can, as a user becomes more compulsive in his behavior, become less about sex and more of an "emotional escape mechanism from mental stress."[28] This online sexual compulsivity is manifesting itself in problems and difficulties for the pornography user, and for the user's spouse and family.

The Effects of Internet Pornography on the Family

Some couples and clinicians claim pornography consumed in a mutual and open manner can be a positive factor for marital intimacy. It must be noted, however, that in most cultural and clinical settings, reported pornography use is neither mutual nor open, but rather a secret and solitary pursuit with the potential for accompanying compulsive and addictive elements.[29]

Survey research conducted by Bridges, Bergner, and Hesson-Mcinnis in 2003 showed married women were significantly more concerned with a partner's online pornography consumption than women in dating relationships. As with any addictive behavior within the context of family relationships, there is some expectation that cybersex addiction may have negative consequences for members of the pornography user's family. Perhaps one of the most informative studies of the impact of Internet sexual addiction on families was conducted by Jennifer P. Schneider.[29] Schneider used qualitative research methods to survey 94 individuals who had a spouse or partner who demonstrated Internet based sexual compulsivity. Of these 94 sexual compulsives, 92 were men.

When asked about the addict's behavior, all of the responses included viewing and, or downloading pornography along with masturbation. Schneider also found that 57 of the addicts did not engage in offline sexual affairs. Only 28 of the respondents reported that their addicted spouse did engage in offline affairs, with 9 reporting an unsure response. In addition, Schneider found that the addicts developed a tolerance to their Internet sexual activities that resulted in an escalation of online sexual behavior including increased amount of time online, a larger number of online partners, bizarre or riskier activities, or going from virtual to actual sexual encounters.[30]

Schneider also noted that cybersex had a significant impact on the non-addicted spouse or partner. Most of the respondents described some combination of devastation, hurt, betrayal, loss of self-esteem, mistrust, suspicion, fear, and a lack of intimacy with their addicted spouses. Of the respondents who had children, the following negative effects were reported. The kids lost parental time and attention due to the parent's compulsive Internet use. Also, a number of the respondents reported that the children witnessed arguments and increased stress in the home because of the addict's behavior. Finally, some of the respondents reported that the children had been exposed to pornography on the computer or witnessed their fathers masturbating while at the computer.[31]

Schneider also discovered that cybersex addiction was a major contributing factor to separation and divorce. Nearly a quarter of the respondents were separated from their spouses and a number were contemplating divorce as a result of the addiction. In addition, in 68% of the couples, one or both of the partners had lost interest in relational sex. Wives in the study tended to compare themselves unfavorably with the online pornography models and felt hopeless about being able to compete with them. Finally, spouses reported overwhelmingly that the Cyber affairs were as emotionally painful to them as live offline affairs and they considered virtual affairs just as much adultery as live affairs.[32]

More men are turning to online sexual behavior, even preferring Internet sexuality to a sexual relationship with a spouse. This compulsive sexual behavior can have negative consequences for the user and his family. Understanding how these behavioral problems evolve may help in developing effective strategies for addressing them.

The Psychological Framework

The psychological framework seeks to understand the issues and problems of Internet pornography within the context of mental processes and psychological factors. According to psychologists, these mental processes and psychological factors hold both the antecedents and solutions to Internet pornography addiction. Effectively dealing with addiction to Internet pornography, involves understanding and addressing the psychological antecedents and the mental processes from which the addiction arises and seeking to change the faulty thinking processes that fuel the addiction.[33]

The psychological framework is at least partially correct. Changing faulty thinking processes is a foundational step in dealing with the problem of Internet pornography.

> *"You took off your former way of life, the old man that is corrupted by deceitful desires; you are being renewed in the spirit of your minds."*
> Ephesians 4:22-23

According to this passage a changed life is possible if individuals will actively put off their old selves and, in so doing, allow God to transform their minds. Effectively addressing the problem of Internet pornography involves teaching people how to be made new in the spirit or attitudes of their minds. In essence, individuals who struggle with Internet pornography must be trained to embrace a new way of thinking that frees their minds from the stranglehold of pornography.[34]

CHAPTER 5
INTERNET PORNOGRAPHY AND WOMEN

In the previous chapters, the discussion concerning Internet pornography and the problems associated with it for the individual, the family, and society, is written from the perspective that men are the primary consumers of Internet pornography. Older research indicates that men have more permissive attitudes toward pornography and are its primary consumers.[1] New studies of Internet pornography viewers, however, may be challenging the assumption that pornography use is entirely a male phenomenon.

In a recent study involving more than 15,000 people, 75% of the men and 41% of women admitted to intentionally viewing or downloading online pornography.[2] Mark Laasar and Patrick Carnes, experts on pornography use and sexual addiction note that in the last 25 years there has been a dramatic increase in the number of women struggling with pornography.[3] Not surprisingly, this is about the length of time that the Internet has made pornography available online. Mark Laasar, who specializes in counseling Christians involved with pornography and sexual addiction, estimates that somewhere between 25-30% of Christian women struggle with pornography as compared to 50-60% for Christian men.[4] While men struggle with pornography at a rate 2 times that of women, the growth of pornography use among women is a significant cause for concern.

The Female Brain and Pornography

When it comes to pornography, as with most areas of life, women are different than men. Men's brains are sexually aroused primarily by visual imagery, especially of the sexual organs and explicit images of sexual acts. Mark Kastleman, who has written extensively on the brain science behind pornography explains that vision, images of the physical act of sex, variety, aggression, and the desire to masturbate are the keys pornographers use to open the male brain to pornography. He also notes that men move through the process of arousal at a lightning fast pace and in doing so they block out thoughts of wife, family, love, career, and anything that might distract them from their total focus on the physical act of sex. [5]

Because of the way the female brain works, pornographers use a different set of keys to open them up to pornography. Women are sexually aroused not by explicit visual imagery but by fantasizing about loving mutual and fulfilling relationships. Pornography producers have gone to great lengths to study the types of content with the potential to turn women into consumers of their products.[6]

One of the most effective ways pornographers use to attract the attention and patronage of women is through cybersex chat rooms. Women are 20% more likely than men to talk about intimacy and sex in a chatroom.[7] The chat room provides a place for intimate discussion and relationship building that many women crave. Kastleman describes how pornographers are using chat rooms to lure women to Internet porn sites. A woman may begin a casual conversation in a chat room that leads to romantic talk. Eventually, as inhibitions are eroded, the conversation may lead to hardcore sexual dialogue. This type of sexually charged discussion combined with perceived relational intimacy can help desensitize the woman, leading her to be more likely to view Internet pornography. Internet pornographers, who understand this progression are now providing online adult meeting rooms and chat rooms that are linked to their sites in hopes of increasing the number of women among their customer base.[8]

Consequences of Pornography Use by Women

Younger women are beginning to use Internet pornography at alarming rates. In a recent study of college students, 88% of the college women surveyed admitted to having viewed pornography.[9] A potentially negative consequence of increased viewing of pornography by women is that they may become more like men with regard to their attitudes and perceptions about sex. Kastleman notes that women who view pornography regularly may develop a more male-like focus on casual sex as a purely physical act. In addition, these women may develop a cycle of arousal that is visually initiated and progresses rapidly. This sexual transformation of women may act to further erode marriages and families as sex continues to suffer loses as an essential component of relational intimacy and bonding between a husband and wife.

Another negative consequence of this transformation is that women are becoming more susceptible to pornography compulsions and addiction.[10] Whether in men or women, pornography addiction, as discussed in the preceding chapter, can have devastating consequences for the addict as well as for the addict's family.

How Pornography affects Women

In recent decades, it was thought that pornography would increase the threat of rape and violence against women. Many experts argue, however, that there is no evidence to support a relationship between pornography and increased incidences of violence or sexual aggression. Regardless, pornography does present a number of threats to women.

There is growing evidence to suggest that Internet pornography contributes to negative body image and decreased self-esteem among women. In a study of the effects of Internet pornography use on spouses, a common theme was that women felt devalued, inadequate, and undesirable when their husbands viewed Internet pornography.[11] Most of the women interviewed in the study felt that they could not compete with the "perfect" Internet models. They felt that their own bodies could never measure up to what their husbands were seeing online. One woman in the study described herself as feeling ugly, worthless, and unwanted.

Most of the women interviewed for the study had all but given up on having fulfilling sexual relationships with their husbands. On the occasions when there was relational sex with their husbands, the wives admitted to thinking that their husbands minds were not really there with them, but focused on the "Internet girls." Pornography deprived these wives the affection and intimacy they deserved from their husbands and led in most cases to separation or divorce.

Along with contributing to negative body image and decreased self-esteem, Internet pornography objectifies women. Pornography portrays women as objects to be used for the sexual gratification of men. Women are viewed as nameless bodies whose value is determined solely by their physical attributes and the ability to perform sexually. Pornography promotes a shameless disregard for women as persons of inherent value and dignity and perpetuates inappropriate attitudes and perceptions about women.

A content analysis of user posts on one Internet pornography site revealed a tendency among pornography users to rate and categorize pornography models by their racial characteristics, age, physical attributes, and ability to perform sexual acts. One man described using a computer spread sheet to catalogue and categorize his thousands of "Porn Stars" and rate them accordingly. Viewing women as sexual objects to be collected, catalogued, and rated is demeaning and inappropriate, and as pornography use becomes more prevalent, objectification of women is becoming more pronounced.

The Biblical View of Women

Genesis 1:27 tells us, "So God created man in His own image, in the image of God He created him: male and female He created them (NIV)." Both men and women are created by God to bear His image and are divinely imbued with great value and dignity. Pornography, by objectifying women, violates God's intentions in creation.

In addition to being created in the image of God, women are highly valued as objects of God's favor and compassion as evidenced in the divine plan of redemption. God placed such a high value on humanity, that He was willing to sacrifice His only Son to secure redemption. With regard to God's plan of salvation both men and women share equally. John 3:16 reveals the depth of God's love and commitment for humanity, "For God so loved the world that he gave his one and only Son, that whoever believes in him shall not perish but have eternal life (NIV)."

CHAPTER 6
INTERNET PORNOGRPAHY AND THE CHURCH

One possible explanation for the use of Internet pornography by Christians might be found in the potency of the Internet's Triple-A-Engine that has proven irresistible to many who have never before struggled with a sexual compulsion. Many Christian men who struggle with Internet pornography would undoubtedly be included in this group. These individuals may have a vulnerability to, or proclivity for, sexual compulsivity, but that they have sufficient internal resources and impulse control to have resisted acting on these behaviors until faced with the power of the Triple-A-Engine.[1]

Christian men in America are increasingly unable to muster the inner resources to control their impulses to view Internet pornography. One reason for this may be found in the American church's growing infatuation with contemporary practices of spirituality that emphasize subjective emotional experiences as a basis for spiritual growth and relationship with God to the exclusion of spirituality that cultivates life transformation and godliness. Peter J. Jankowski, Professor of Psychology at Bethel University, describes the problem with these spiritual practices which he calls postmodern spirituality:

Postmodern spirituality tends to (a) neglect the importance of doctrine in providing meaning, thus devaluing the cognitive dimension of spirituality; (b) overemphasize subjective experience, making only "felt experience" authoritative, thereby lessening the importance of exercising faith as a way of knowing; and (c) disconnect people from each other and, in so doing, inhibit closer communion with God and neglect the inseparable responsibility of meeting other persons' needs. "Postmodern spirituality seems to alter the three components of spirituality that have been found to help people make changes in their lives and overcome difficulties."[2]

Jankowski relates subjective centered postmodern spirituality with an inability to deal with life's problems and make meaningful life changes. He recommends a process that moves a person toward a resilient spirituality that fosters inner spiritual transformation and life change. This process includes reemphasizing theology and doctrine, building spiritual community, and strengthening a person's relationship with God.[3]

In order to build spiritual resiliency into a person's life, Jankowski recommends, among other things, practicing Christian spiritual disciplines. Jankowski refers to Dallas Willard's work on the subject for examples of these spiritual disciplines: solitude and silence, prayer, fasting, meditation, reading and studying sacred writings, fellowship, worship, and confession of wrongdoings to one another and to God.[4] In recent history, however, the American church has placed little emphasis on the practice of spiritual disciplines and their role in transforming a person's life. Considering the apparent weakness of the American church, which claims so many conversions but has less and less impact on the culture, with Christians virtually indistinguishable from the world, Willard postulates that the teaching focus of the church may be at least partially responsible.[5] The contemporary American church, according to Willard, tends to embrace either a right leaning conservative gospel that focuses on regeneration as a work of God to get people to heaven, or a left leaning contemporary social ethic that functions as a substitute for traditional church doctrine. In either case, limited attention is given to the work of God in supplying the necessary spiritual resources to live life in an intimate, personal, and interactive relationship with Him—experiencing the abundant life of His kingdom even in a present earthly reality.[6]

A Biblical View of Pornography

The discussion of pornography is for many people uncomfortable, and rightly so. Pornography is a deviation of God's plan for human sexuality, and is both harmful to the human condition and prohibited according to the teachings of Scripture. Pornography, especially as mediated through the Internet is, however, a very real and significant problem in America and must be addressed. In addition, the issue of Internet pornography use by Christians is a particular problem that demands a reasoned and responsible dialogue from a theological as well as a social perspective. As with any dialogue of this nature, the Bible is the most appropriate place to begin.

Porneia

The word "pornography" comes from the Greek word porneia, which refers to a range of behaviors from prostitution, fornication, unchastity, harlotry, whoremongering, and homosexuality. "The general impression one receives from reading the New Testament literature is that porneia represents a general phrase representing every kind of sexual immorality".[7] Paul used porneia in 1 Corinthians 5:1 to describe the sexual sin to which Corinthian Christians were turning a blind eye.

The word pornography comes from the combination of porneia with the Greek word for writing, graphos. Thus, pornography means literally, the writing about or depicting of sexual immorality.[8] Mark Laaser provides a definition of pornography that has been accepted in the field of clinical counseling, "Pornography can be defined as writing about, or displaying in some medium—

magazines, videos, television, movies, the Internet—nudity or sexual activity that excites sexual feeling".[9]

Pornography as Sin

From a Christian perspective, the practice of using sexually explicit material to excite sexual feeling represents unhealthy, immoral, and sinful activity. In Matthew 5:28 Jesus clearly condemned the use of pornography when He stated that lusting after a woman was comparable to the sin of adultery. In addition, the use of pornography should be regarded as sinful because it represents applauding wickedness, is damaging to the marital relationship, may lead to habituation and compulsivity, and is often accompanied by lying and deceitful behavior.

Applauding Wickedness

Pornography not only causes a person to commit the sin of lust, but often depicts or describes adultery, fornication, homosexuality, rape, incest, and other overtly sinful behaviors. Romans 1:26-32, 1 Timothy 1:8-11, 1 Thessalonians 4:3-5, and numerous other Bible passages condemn the very acts depicted and promoted in pornography. The first chapter of Romans warns those who not only practice wickedness, but those giving their approval to such wickedness: " Although they know God's righteous decree that those who do such things deserve death, they not only continue to do these very things but also approve of those who practice them." Romans 1:32 (NIV). The intentional viewing of pornography involves the willing acceptance and approval of the sinful acts it depicts, which is clearly contrary to the teaching of Scripture and constitutes the sin of applauding wickedness.

Theologian, Everett F. Harrison, describes applauding wickedness found in Romans 1:32 as a crowning offense against God. Instead of repenting of their own sins, those who applaud wickedness promote wrongdoing and encourage others toward sin and revolt against God.[10] Another theologian, C. E. B. Cranfield, adds that those who condone and applaud the sinful actions of others are actually contributing to the establishment of sinful behavior in the community and influencing public opinion to accept immorality resulting in further and more widespread corruption.[11]

Viewing pornography is an offense against God because it promotes rebellion against God and encourages sexual immorality. In addition, it encourages, in the individual and in society, the types of wanton immoral behavior it depicts, and leads to even greater tolerance and acceptance of sexual sin. Viewing pornography is an act of applauding wickedness, and as such is warned against and condemned by God's word.

Damaging Marital Relationships

In addition to applauding wickedness, recent research indicates that using pornography decreases sexual intimacy and damages marital relationships.[12] In Ephesians 6:22-33 God calls men to love and protect their wives and to unite completely with them, becoming one flesh. Pornography interferes with this uniting process, keeping husbands and wives from fully experiencing God's plan in marriage. Ephesians 5:31 describes the sanctity and unity of the marital relationship "For this reason a man will leave his father and mother and be united to his wife, and the two will become one flesh (NIV)." A. Skevington Wood describes the biblical notion of becoming one flesh:

> *This union refers to sexual intercourse which is thus hallowed by the approval of God Himself. It is because of this exalted biblical view of marital relations that the church has taken its stand on the indissolubility of the marital bond and the impermissibility of polygamy, adultery, or divorce.*[13]

It is difficult to imagine that an individual could be involved with the intentional use of pornography for the purpose of exciting sexual feelings and not violate the sanctity of the one flesh principle in marriage. Richard Land, president of the Ethics and Religious Liberty Commission of the Southern Baptist Convention writes,

> *Pornography perverts and distorts all of the God-given purposes for sexual intimacy. Pornography teaches people to disrespect the sanctity of marriage and the one flesh concept. It teaches people to disregard the intimacy of knowing another person by encouraging sexual intercourse as a casual relationship. Sex is viewed as a form of recreation with superficial self-gratification. Pornography also teaches self-gratification without regard for the welfare of one's sexual partner. It is narcissistic and self-centered.*[14]

A recent study of the effects of Internet pornography use on the spouse of the user concludes:

> *The devastating emotional impact of a cybersex affair is described by many partners as similar if not the same as that of a real affair. The partner's self-esteem may be damaged; strong feelings of hurt, betrayal, abandonment, devastation, loneliness, shame, isolation, humiliation, and jealously are evoked.*[15]

Pornography use is damaging to the marriage relationship. It damages the well-being of one's spouse and denies God's plan for marriage by disrespecting and violating the one flesh concept.

Habituation and Compulsivity

Pornography can also become habitual and controlling. Research indicates that pornography is often associated with compulsive and addictive behaviors that may exert a level of control over a person's life.[16] Scripture teaches that Christians are not to participate in behaviors that may control them but to live according to the Holy Spirit's leading and a desire to glorify God. Romans 6: 11-14 reads,

> *In the same way, count yourselves dead to sin but alive to God in Christ Jesus. Therefore do not let sin reign in your mortal body so that you obey its*

> *evil desires. Do not offer the parts of your body to sin, as instruments of wickedness, but rather offer yourselves to God, as those who have been brought from death to life; and offer the parts of your body to him as instruments of righteousness. For sin shall not be your master, because you are not under law, but under grace.*
>
> *Romans 6:11-14 (NIV)*

Paul, in this passage, urges believers to resolve to live their lives by means of God's grace, not being mastered by sinful behavior, but offering themselves to God as willing instruments of His glory and righteousness.[17] A person under the compulsion of addictive influences of pornography, is not able to offer himself fully to God as a willing instrument, and is therefore behaving in a way contrary to God's word.

Lies and Deceit

Finally, viewing pornography is often a solitary and secretive act, involving lying and deceitful behavior. In a study of the impact of compulsive cybersex behaviors on the family, Jennifer P. Schneider found that lying and deceitful behavior commonly accompany Internet pornography use in attempts by the pornography user to conceal his activities. A common response by spouses and partners in relationships with pornography users is reflected in the following statement: "Cybersex results in lying, hiding one's activities, and covering up, and the lies are often the most painful part of an affair".[18] The Bible prohibits lying and deceitful behavior: Ephesians 4:25; Colossians 3:1; and Revelation 21:27 and 25:15 regard such behavior as inappropriate for Christian relationships. Lying and deceitful behavior are even more egregious in the context of the marriage relationship.

The Real Issue

Pornography represents applauding wickedness, is damaging to the marital relationship, may lead to habituation and compulsivity, and is often accompanied by lying and deceitful behavior. When understood in this light, there is no other way to view pornography, but through the framework of sin. Accepting the sin framework for pornography is the best starting place for developing a solution for it. Contemporary views of pornography in America, at least among secular clinicians and researchers, focus on pornography as a freedom of speech issue, an adult issue, a psychological issue, or a social issue. These views all bring a level of understanding to the debate surrounding Internet pornography, but they fail to address the core issue; pornography in all its forms, must be viewed as sin. The good thing about accepting the sin framework for pornography is that there is a solution:

> *For we know that our old self was crucified with him so that the body of sin might be done away with, that we should no longer be slaves to sin-- because anyone who has died has been freed from sin. Now if we died with Christ, we believe that we will also live with him. For we know that since Christ was raised from the dead, he cannot die again; death no longer has mastery over him.*
> *The death he died, he died to sin once for all; but the life he lives, he lives to God.*
> Romans 6:6-10 (NIV)

According to God's word, pornography—as is true with all sin—will lose its influence when Christians are able to consider themselves dead to it, but alive to God in Christ Jesus. This process of considering oneself dead to sin involves active participation on the part of the Christian through yielding oneself to God in obedience and faith.

CHAPTER 7
GODLY LEADERSHIP

In recent years, the problem of Internet pornography has been growing largely unchecked. There are some in the church and in society who are beginning to recognize that this problem needs addressing, but there are seemingly too few leaders who are willing to take on the challenge. If the church is to have a significant impact on the problem of Internet pornography, it will take Godly leadership.

Remember the story of Caleb. The Israelites were living in the promised land but they had not yet dealt with the descendants of Anak, who had entrenched themselves in fortified cities in the hill country of Hebron. Caleb recognized the need for leadership and he took up the challenge. Caleb drove the sons of Anak from Hebron and claimed it as his inheritance, just as Moses promised. Hebron, under the leadership of Caleb, became a stronghold of faithfulness to God.

Contrast the story of Caleb with the story of the sons of Benjamin. When the sons of Benjamin were given the land of Jerusalem as their inheritance, the Jebusites occupied the region. God told His people in Exodus 23:24 to completely overthrow the inhabitants of the land and to remain separate from them, but the Sons of Benjamin did not do what God said. No leader rose to take on the challenge of the Jebusites, and God's people lived together with them in the land. In time, the Sons of Benjamin were led astray to worship the false god's of the Jebusites. This disobedience by the Sons of Benjamin angered God and brought His judgment on them. Because Caleb trusted God and was willing to take up the call of leadership, his land and his descendants were spared the troubles experienced by the sons of Benjamin. The success of the Israelites in the promised-land depended on godly and effective leadership, and the people suffered when that leadership was lacking.

Just as He did in the time of Caleb, God is calling leaders to take a stand against the enemies that threaten His people. God is calling leaders to take a stand against Internet pornography. Taking a stand against Internet pornography will not be an easy task, but we can gain valuable insight for dealing with this problem by understanding the life and the actions of Caleb as he dealt with the giant descendants of Anak.

Caleb Followed God Wholeheartedly

Caleb was serious about obeying God. He trusted God completely and submitted himself to God's commands. In Numbers 14:24, God describes Caleb as a man who has a different spirit from the rest of his generation: a man who followed God wholeheartedly. Caleb trusted God to do what He said, and believed that God would indeed see His people through any difficulty and deliver them safely into the promised-land. Caleb was sold out completely to God and his life and his leadership reflected that commitment.

To confront the challenge of Internet pornography, we need a generation of Calebs. We need leaders who follow God wholeheartedly, who take their call seriously, and whose lives reflect that level of commitment. If current estimates are correct, as many as 60 percent of Christian men struggle with Internet pornography. In addition, nearly 30 percent of pastors are having significant moral failures in this area. In many cases, church leadership is compromised, and because of this, God's people suffer.

Even in many churches where leaders are not experiencing moral failure with Internet pornography, there is an unwillingness to take a bold and decisive stand against it. Too few church leaders are willing to put their credibility on the line, step out of their comfort zones, and deal with the giant. Internet pornography has gone unchallenged in the church for too long and it is time for God's called leaders to take a stand.

Taking a stand against Internet pornography will require leaders who are willing to deal with their own moral failures first. Taking a stand requires repentance. Pastors and church leaders who have experienced moral failure with Internet pornography or other sexual sin must repent and do whatever is necessary to provide appropriate spiritual leadership for their congregations. In some cases this might require a leader's submitting to counseling or an accountability relationship. Other cases might require a leader to remove himself from leadership until the appropriate steps of restoration can be accomplished.

Pastors and church leaders who have not been compromised by moral failure may also need to repent. The church is being ravaged by Internet pornography and too few leaders seem willing to do anything about it. The people of God have been left unprotected and in some cases, it is because their shepherds have not been diligent.

During the Old Testament days of Nehemiah, the walls surrounding Jerusalem were allowed to crumble and the people of God were left unprotected from their enemies. When Nehemiah heard that his people were left unprotected and harassed, he wept and he repented. Nehemiah repented for his own lack of diligence and for that of his people for failing to uphold the commands, laws, and decrees of God.

Nehemiah, like Caleb, was a leader who followed God wholeheartedly. He made sure that he was personally right with God and then he acted. This is the type of leadership that is needed to confront Internet pornography in the church today: leaders who follow God wholeheartedly, who are willing to repent of their shortcomings, then take bold and decisive action.

CHAPTER 8
TAKE ACTION

The church and its leaders must take action and deal with the problem of Internet pornography. Caleb was a man who followed God wholeheartedly and not only knew what needed to be done, but was willing to take the necessary action. In dealing with the giants that threatened God's people, Caleb demonstrated an effective strategy that we can also use.

Take God at His Word

Caleb took God at His word. Caleb knew what God said, and he charted the course of his life by God's word.

Caleb heard the message of God, that He would deliver His people into the Promised Land, and he believed it. Even when circumstances made it seem impossible, Caleb lived out his trust in God.

The story of Caleb and the people of Israel gives us a powerful example to follow for taking action in the fight against Internet pornography. First, we must take God completely at His word. We must take God at His word with regard to the sinfulness of Internet pornography. Christians, especially church leaders, must view Internet pornography with the same seriousness that God views it.

Joshua Chapter 7, recounts the story of Achan. Achan was a soldier in Israel's army. After Israel experienced victory in battle against Jericho, Achan took from the battle some of the spoils that God commanded the people not to take. No one in Israel knew about the things Achan took, but God knew. Later, Israel went to battle once again, but this time they did not experience victory. Instead, they were defeated, humiliated, and forced to flee for their lives. God told Joshua, the leader of Israel, that it was because of the sin of Achan that Israel was weak and powerless against its enemies.

God viewed Achan's sin as a serious matter, and He was not willing to simply overlook the transgression. Before God would again empower His people, the sin had to be dealt with, and the responsibility for dealing with Achan's sin fell on Joshua. The Bible tells us that Joshua dealt harshly with Achan, putting him and his family to death.

God would not tolerate sin in the midst of His covenant people. The sin had to be dealt with and it had to be stopped. Sin like Achan's, left unchecked, would run rampant through Israel, prohibiting the nation from accomplishing its covenant purpose of demonstrating God's glory to the world.

Currently, the sin of Internet pornography remains largely unchallenged among God's people. In order for the church, as God's covenant people, to demonstrate God's glory to the world, it must deal with the sin of Internet pornography. God can restore strength and power to His people and enable us to live in victory, but we must take this sin seriously and deal with it effectively. Some Christians are calling Internet pornography the "new norm" in the church. We cannot accept this as the norm. God definitely does not accept pornography use as the norm for His people and neither should we:

> *Put to death, therefore, whatever belongs to your earthly nature: sexual immorality, impurity, lust, evil desires and greed, which is idolatry. Because of these, the wrath of God is coming.*
>
> Colossians 3:5-6 (NIV)

Raise The Spiritual Standard

In addition to taking God at His word, Caleb raised the spiritual standard in his life and inspired those around him to do likewise. Caleb walked in obedience to God and his example encouraged others. Caleb was not willing to settle for less than complete obedience to God:

> *"Now then, just as the Lord promised, he has kept me alive for forty-five years since the time he said this to Moses, while Israel moved about in the desert. So here I am today, eighty-five years old! I am still as strong today as the day Moses sent me out; I'm just as vigorous to go out to battle now as I was then. Now give me this hill country that the Lord promised me that day. You yourself heard then that the Anakites were there and their cities were large and fortified, but, the Lord helping me, I will drive them out just as he said." Then Joshua blessed Caleb son of Jephunneh and gave him Hebron as his inheritance. So Hebron has belonged to Caleb son of Jephunneh*

the Kenizzite ever since, because he followed the Lord, the God of Israel, wholeheartedly.
Joshua 14:10-14 (NIV)

God blessed Caleb's obedience by giving him Hebron as his inheritance, and by establishing it as a stronghold of faith for generations.

We must raise the spiritual standard in our own lives, our families, and our churches. Like Caleb, we can strive to live in complete obedience to God, or we can settle for something less.

If we will raise the spiritual standard, God will enable us to have victory in this battle. Here are some suggestions for raising the spiritual standard:

1. Read God's word daily. Learn how to read and journal on God's word. Spend time each day submitting yourself to God's word and letting it transform your heart and mind. See the appendix 2 on using the SOAP daily Bible study method.

2. Memorize Scripture. Renew your mind by memorizing passages of Scripture and using them to defeat temptation when it arises.

3. Practice confession and repentance. I john 1:8-9 reads: *If we say, "We have no sin," we are deceiving ourselves, and the truth is not in us.*

If we confess our sins, He is faithful and righteous to forgive us our sins and to cleanse us from all unrighteousness. (HCSB).

We must find the right time and place to confess the sin of pornography. This might be with an accountability partner or in a small group gathering. Then, we must turn from that sin and uplift one another as we each seek to walk in obedience to Christ.

Don't Give In

Caleb was persistent. He had a goal in mind—to take the hill country that God promised him—and he would not give in. In dealing with the problem of Internet pornography, we must have this same persistence. Philippians 1:6 tells us that God will complete the good work that He began in us. We must take God at his word and continue to trust Him that He will work in us and through us if we will yield our lives to Him.

Whether we are struggling with Internet Pornography ourselves, or we are encouraging others who are in the midst of this struggle, we must never, never, never, give in. Instead of accepting Internet pornography as the norm, we should embrace a new norm for spirituality and for obedience and faithfulness in the Christian life, as is encouraged in God's word:

> *Therefore, since we are surrounded by such a great cloud of witnesses, let us throw off everything that hinders and the sin that so easily entangles, and let us run with perseverance the race marked out for us. Let us fix our eyes on Jesus, the author and perfecter of our faith, who for the joy set before him endured the cross, scorning its shame, and sat down at the right hand of the throne of God. Consider him who endured such opposition from sinful men, so that you will not grow weary and lose heart.*
> Hebrews 12:1-3 (NIV)

APPENDIX 1
"S"

Try Harder by "S"

1000's of them in the bed,

the ghosts, no not ghosts,

real perfect fantasy women,

airbrushed, body parts,

disconnected willing to do anything,

I cannot compete,

they won't leave,

he's invited them in

compared and found lacking,

numbness, wishing I was dead

violated, I'm not my own,

The silence screams

feel him watching me, waiting

waiting for me to be fixed

then all will be well,

No, No is screaming in my head.

I'm real, I hurt, I am me.

Feeling insane and crazy

But I'm sane,

Try harder. NO I don't want to.

I am me. I am enough. I am enough.

"S"

"S" asked me to tell her story because it is the story of thousands of women whose husbands are addicted to pornography.

I am the wife of 30 years to a good man-- in many ways, a Christian man and former church deacon who is addicted to porn, who allowed porn to turn him into a selfish and an emotionally and sexually abusive man. (He is no longer abusive as I have developed boundaries, sought counseling, and even left him 3 times). But our marriage has been devastated by Internet pornography and singles-dating sites, and we are talking about divorce.

I personally have sought counseling from probably 3-4 pastors and church leaders who regularly counsel. Plus we have been thru a 'deliverance' session. Not one pastor or church leader would directly and firmly confront my husband's porn use. It was like they were embarrassed, it was a sacred subject, it was implied that I was perhaps overreacting. It's like they slapped his wrists and then looked at me to go home and make him happy in bed and all would be well.

Lack of understanding, lack of support from so called experienced counselors and pastors was extremely destructive to me. It made me feel it was my fault and made me question my sanity and perception of events. This on top of the denial, blame shifting and lying from my husband. It is by the grace of God and groups such as NLP and finally one counselor—a Christian—who called things as they were and didn't sugar coat it, that I am healthy and working my way to wholeness today despite the state of my marriage.

I believe our society has so watered down the word "porn' that it isn't even shocking anymore...

APPENDIX 2
SOAP: DAILY BIBLE STUDY METHOD

Reading God's word each day is a vital part of walking with Christ and developing a resilient spirituality that can help a person overcome life's temptations and struggles. The SOAP Bible study method can help us become consistent in daily Bible intake and applying God's word to life.

SOAP Bible study involves reading a Scripture passage each day, then writing down observations and applications for life based on an understanding of that passage. SOAP is an acronym that guides us through 4 essential steps of daily Bible study: Scripture, Observation, Application, and Prayer. Here is a summary of the SOAP Bible study method:

Scripture: Open your Bible to the daily reading passage. Read the passage and allow God to speak to you through His word. Look for a short passage or verse that speaks to you in a particular way and write it in the **S** section of your journal.

Observation: What does this passage mean? What principles is the passage teaching. What is God saying to you through this passage? Write what the passage means in your own words in **O** section of your journal.

Application: Personalize what you have read by asking yourself how it applies to your life. What actions do you need to take in your life based on what you have learned from this passage. Write this down in the **A** section of your journal.

Prayer: In your journal, write a prayer to God. This can be as simple as asking God to help you use this scripture in your life, or it may be a greater insight on what He is revealing to you. Remember, prayer is a two way conversation. Be sure to listen to what God is saying and write it in the **P** section of your journal.

A 14 day reading plan and journal is provided to get started with SOAP. Once you finish this plan, use a notebook, or a computer to create additional pages. This is the front line in the battle against Internet pornography. Even if you are not personally struggling with Internet pornography, your daily Bible study will raise the spiritual standard in your own life and encourage those around you to do likewise. We MUST hold this line!

14 Day Reading Plan

Day 1	1 Thessalonians 4:1-8
Day 2	1 Corinthians 10:1-13
Day 3	Romans 6:1-14
Day 4	1 Corinthians 6:12-20
Day 5	Colossians 3:1-10
Day 6	Galatians 5:16-25
Day 7	Matthew 5:27-30
Day 8	1 John 2:15-17
Day 9	Romans 5:1-11
Day 10	1 John 1:5-10
Day 11	Romans 7:13-25
Day 12	Ephesians 1:15-23
Day 13	Ephesians 2:1-10
Day 14	Philippians 3:1-11

Bible Passage _____ Date _____

S: _____

_____

_____

O: _____

_____

_____

_____

_____

A: _____

_____

_____

_____

P: _____

_____

_____

DEALING WITH GIANTS

Bible Passage _____ Date _____

S: _____

_____

_____

O: _____

_____

_____

_____

_____

_____

A: _____

_____

_____

_____

P: _____

_____

_____

Bible Passage _____ Date _____

S: _____

_____

_____

O: _____

_____

_____

_____

_____

_____

A: _____

_____

_____

_____

P: _____

_____

_____

DEALING WITH GIANTS

Bible Passage _____ Date _____

S: _____

_____

_____

O: _____

_____

_____

_____

_____

_____

A: _____

_____

_____

_____

P: _____

_____

_____

Bible Passage _____ Date _____

S: _____

O: _____

A: _____

P: _____

DEALING WITH GIANTS

Bible Passage _____ Date _____

S: _____

_____

_____

O: _____

_____

_____

_____

_____

_____

A: _____

_____

_____

_____

P: _____

_____

_____

TONY HOFFMAN

Bible Passage _____ Date _____

S: _____

_____

_____

O: _____

_____

_____

_____

_____

A: _____

_____

_____

_____

P: _____

_____

_____

DEALING WITH GIANTS

Bible Passage _____ Date _____

S: _____

_____

_____

O: _____

_____

_____

_____

_____

_____

A: _____

_____

_____

_____

P: _____

_____

_____

TONY HOFFMAN

Bible Passage _____ Date _____

S: _____

_____

_____

O: _____

_____

_____

_____

_____

A: _____

_____

_____

P: _____

_____

_____

DEALING WITH GIANTS

Bible Passage _____ Date _____

S: _____

_____

_____

O: _____

_____

_____

_____

_____

A: _____

_____

_____

_____

P: _____

_____

_____

Bible Passage _____ Date _____

S: _____

_____

_____

O: _____

_____

_____

_____

_____

_____

A: _____

_____

_____

_____

P: _____

_____

_____

DEALING WITH GIANTS

Bible Passage _____ Date _____

S: _____

_____

_____

O: _____

_____

_____

_____

_____

_____

A: _____

_____

_____

_____

P: _____

_____

_____

Bible Passage _____ Date _____

S: _____

_____

_____

O: _____

_____

_____

_____

_____

_____

A: _____

_____

_____

_____

P: _____

_____

_____

DEALING WITH GIANTS

Bible Passage _____ Date _____

S: _____

_____

_____

O: _____

_____

_____

_____

_____

_____

A: _____

_____

_____

_____

P: _____

_____

_____

NOTES

Chapter 1: Dealing With Giants

1. internetworldstatistics.com

2. Griffin-Shelley, Eric. 2003. The Internet and sexuality: A literature review—1993-2002. *Sexual and Relationship Therapy* 18 (August): 355.

3. Cooper, Al, Eric Griffin-Shelley, David L. Delmonico, and Robin M. Mathy. 2001. Online sexual problems: Assessment and predictive variables. *Sexual Addiction and Compulsivity* 8 (3): 268.

4. Mark B. Kastleman, The *Drug of the New Millenium*, 3.

5. Gardner, C. J. 2001. Tangled in the worst of the web. *Christianity Today* 45 (4): 42-49.

6. Abell, Jesse W., Timothy A. Steenbergh, and Michael J. Boivin. 2006. Cyperporn use in the context of religiosity. *Journal of Psychology and Theology* 34 (2): 168.

7. Cooper, Al ed. 1998. Sexuality and the Internet: Surfing into the new millennium. *Cyberpsychology and Behavior* 1: 187-93.

8. Melton, J. Gordon, ed. 1989. *The church speak on: Pornography*. Detroit, MI: Gale Research Inc., xxi

9. Melton, J. Gordon, ed. 1989, v-vii.

Chapter 2: A Brief History of Pornography in America

1. Slade, Joseph W. 2001. A brief history of American pornography. In *Pornography and sexual representation: A reference guide,* 3: 39. Westport CT: Greenwood Press.

2. Slade, Joseph W. 2001. 40

3. Ibid.

4. Ibid.

5. Slade, Joseph W. 2001. 41.

6. Ibid.

7. Slade, Joseph W. 2001. 43

8. Slade, Joseph W. 2001. 46.

9. Ibid.

10. Roth, John K., ed. 1997. Pornography. In *Encyclopedia of social issues*, vol. 5. Tarrytown, NY: Marshall Cavendish, 1234

11. Ibid.

12. Slade, Joseph W. 2001, 67.

13. Rist, Ray C. 1975. *The pornography controversy: Changing moral standards in American life.* New Brunswick, NJ: Transaction Books, 41-42

14. Randall, Richard S. 1989. *Freedom and taboo: Pornography and the politics of a self divided*. Berkeley, CA: University of California Press.

15. Slade, Joseph W. 2001, 69.

16. Rist, Ray C. 1975. 65.

17. Melton, J. Gordon, ed. 1989. *The church speak on: Pornography*. Detroit, MI: Gale Research Inc., xvii

18. Idem xviii

Chapter 3: The Next Sexual Revolution

1. Cooper, Al. 2002 . *Sex and the Internet: a guidebook for clinicians.* New York, NY: Brunner-Routledge.

2. Griffin-Shelley, Eric. 2003. The Internet and sexuality: A literature review—1993-2002. *Sexual and Relationship Therapy* 18 (August): 35

3. Cooper, Al ed. 1998. Sexuality and the Internet: Surfing into the new millennium. *Cyberpsychology and Behavior* 1: 187-93.

4. internetworldstatistics.com

5. Dark Reading, 2006. Filters fail to block sexually explicit material. Retrieved March 2007 from http://www.darkreading.com

6. Kaiser Family Foundation, 2002.. *Teens online.* Retrieved March 2007 from http://www.kff.org

7. Carnes, Patrick, 2001. *Out of the shadows: understanding sexual addiction.* Center City, MN: Hazelden: 81.

8. Sabina, Chiara; Janis Wolak; and David Finkelhor, 2008. The nature and dynamics of Internet Pornography exposure for youth. *Cyberpsychology and behavior* 11(6):691-93.

9. Huson, Jerry D. 2005. The experience of male undergraduate Christian college students with pornography: How is disrupts the educational process and spiritual formation. Ph.D. diss. Biola University: 58-9

10. Ibid.

11. Ibid.

Chapter 4: The Problem of Internet Pornography

1. Buzzell, Timothy; Drew Foss, and Zack Middleton, 2006. Explaining use of online pornography: A test of self-control theory and opportunities for deviance. *Journal of criminal justice and popular culture* 13(2): 96-116.

2. Stack, Steven; Ira Wasserman; and Roger Kern, 2004. Adult social bonds and use of Internet pornography. *Social science quarterly* 85 (March): 75-88.

3. Fisher, William A. and Azy Barak, 2001. Internet pornography: A social psychological perspective on Internet sexuality. *The journal of sex research* 38(4):312+

4. Griffin-Shelley, Eric. 2003. The Internet and sexuality: A literature review—1993-2002. *Sexual and Relationship Therapy* 18 (August): 362.

5. Morgan, Timothy C., 2008. Porn's Stranglehold. *Christianity Today* 52(3): 7

6. Griffin-Shelley, Eric. 2003.

7. Fisher, William A. and Azy Barak, 2001.

8. Ibid.

9. Ibid.

10. Poldrack, Russell, 2009. Multitasking: The Brain Seeks Novelty. Posted: October 28, 2009. http://www.huffingtonpost.com

11. Griffiths, Mark, 2001. Sex on the Internet: Observations and implications for Internet sex addiction. *The Journal of Sex Research* 38(4): 333+

12. Ibid.

13. Young, Kimberly, 1999. Internet addiction: Evaluation and treatment. *Student British medical journal* 7: 351-52.

14. Griffiths, Mark, 2001.

15. Ibid.

16. Laaser, Mark, 2004. Healing the wounds of sexual addiction. Grand Rapids, MI: Zondervan.

17. Huson, Jerry D. 2005. The experience of male undergraduate Christian college students with porno-graphy: How is disrupts the educational process and spiritual formation. Ph.D. diss. Biola University

18. Ibid.

19. Ibid.

20. Ibid.

21. Ibid.

22. Sabina, Chiara; Janis Wolak; and David Finkelhor, 2008. The nature and dynamics of Internet Pornography exposure for youth. *Cyberpsychology and behavior* 11(6):691-93.

23. Naomi Wolf, 2003. The porn myth. *The New York Magazine*: October 20   http://nymag.com

24. Young, Kimberly S., Eric Griffin-Shelley, Al Cooper, James O'Mara, and Jennifer Buchanan. 2000. Online infidelity: A new dimension in couple relationships with implications for evaluation and treatment. *In Cybersex: The dark side of the force*, ed. Al Cooper, 31-58. Philadelphia, PA: Brunner-Routledge.

25. Ibid.

26. Schneider, Jennifer P. 2000. Effects of cybersex addiction on the family: Results of a Survey. *In Cybersex: The dark side of the force*, ed. Al Cooper, 31-58. Philadelphia, PA: Brunner-Routledge.

27. Young et al. 2000.

28. Young et al. 2000.

29. Manning, Jill C. 2006. The impact of Internet pornography on marriage and the family: A review of the research. *Sexual addiction and compulsivity* 13 (2-3): 131-65.

30. Schneider, Jennifer P. 2000

31. Ibid.

32. Ibid.

33. Griffiths, Mark, 2001.

34. Morgan, Timothy C., 2008.

Chapter 5: Internet Pornography and Women

1. Fisher, W. A. & Byrne, D. (1978). Sex differences in response to erotica? Love versus lust. Journal of Personality and Social Psychology, 36, 117–125.

2. Albright, Julie M, 2008. Sex in America Online: An Exploration of Sex, Marital Status, and Sexual Identity in Internet Sex Seeking and Its Impacts *Journal of sex research*, 45(2), 175–186.

3. Mark R. Laasar and Patrick Carnes, "Sexual Addiction:", Christian Counseling Today, Vol. 16, No. 1

4. Ibid

5. Mark Kastleman, How Internet Pornographers Market to Men vs. Women http://www.netnanny.com

6. Ibid

7. Albright, Julie M, 2008. Sex in America Online: An Exploration of Sex, Marital Status, and Sexual Identity in Internet Sex Seeking and Its Impacts *Journal of sex research*, 45(2), 175–186.

8. Mark Kastleman, How Internet Pornographers Market to Men vs. Women http://www.netnanny.com

9. O'Reilly, Sarah, Knox, David, Zusman, Marty E, College students attitudes toward pornography use. *College Student Journal*, Jun2007, Vol. 41 Issue 2, p402-406.

10. Mark Kastleman. How Internet Pornographers Market to Men vs. Women http://www.netnanny.com

11. Jennifer P. Schneider "The New Elephant in the Living Room: Effects of compulsive Cybersex Behaviors on the Spouse." *In sex and the Internet: A Guidebook for clinicians* Ed. By Al Cooper, Routledge Taylor and Francis Group, 2002. P.176

Chapter 6

1. Cooper, Al, Eric Griffin-Shelley, David L. Delmonico, and Robin M. Mathy. 2001. Online sexual Problems: Assessment and predictive variables. *Sexual Addiction and Compulsivity* 8 (3): 267-85.

2. Jankowski, Peter J. 2002. Postmodern spirituality: Implications for promoting change. *Counseling and Values* 47 (1): 69.

3. Ibid.

4. Ibid.

5. Willard, Dallas. 1991. *Spirit of the disciplines: Understanding how God changes lives*. San Francisco, CA: Harper Collins

6. Ibid.

7. Patterson, Paige. 1983. *The troubled triumphant church: An exposition of First Corinthians.* Dallas, TX: Criswell Publications.

8. Ibid.

9. Laaser, Mark R. 2004. *Healing the wounds of sexual addiction.* Grand Rapids, MI: Zondervan.

10. Harrison, F. Everett. 1976. *Romans.* In Vol. 10 of *The expositor's Bible commentary.* Edited by Frank Gabelein Grand Rapids, MI: Zondervan.

11. Emerton, J. A., and C. E. B. Cranfield. 1975. *The epistle to the Romans.* Vol. 1. The International Critical Commentary. Edinburgh: T. and T. Clark Limited.

12. Schneider, Jennifer P. 2000. Effects of cybersex addiction on the family: Results of a Survey. In *Cybersex: The dark side of the force*, ed. Al Cooper, 31-58. Philadelphia, PA: Brunner-Routledge.

13. Wood, A. Skevington. 1978. *Ephesians.* In Vol. 11 of *The expositor's Bible commentary.* Edited by Frank Gabelein. Grand Rapids, MI: Zondervan.

14. Land, Richard. 2002. *For faith and family: Changing America by strengthening the Family.* Nashville, TN: Broadman and Holman.

15. Jennifer P. Schneider "The New Elephant in the Living Room: Effects of compulsive Cybersex Behaviors on the Spouse." *In sex and the Internet: A Guidebook for clinicians* Ed. By Al Cooper, Routledge Taylor and Francis Group, 2002. P.176

16. Griffiths, Mark, 2001. Sex on the Internet: Observations and implications for Internet sex addiction. *The Journal of Sex Research* 38(4): 333+

17. Harrison, F. Everett. 1976. *Romans*. In Vol. 10 of *The expositor's Bible commentary.* Edited by Frank Gabelein Grand Rapids, MI: Zondervan.

18. Schneider, Jennifer P. 2000.

ABOUT THE AUTHOR

Tony Hoffman served churches in Florida and Georgia in the areas of Children and Family Ministries and as an Associate Pastor. Tony met Teresa—the love of his life—in college and they were married in 1991. Tony and Teresa have 4 children: Luke, Jonathan, Emma, and Annie. Tony has a Master's and a Doctor's degree in Christian Education and has spent years researching the impact of Internet pornography on the American Church.

Made in the USA
Lexington, KY
09 February 2012